Spat

poems by

Lois Marie Harrod

Finishing Line Press
Georgetown, Kentucky

Copyright © 2021 by Lois Marie Harrod
ISBN 978-1-64662-491-1 First Edition
All rights reserved under International and Pan-American Copyright Conventions. No part of this book may be reproduced in any manner whatsoever without written permission from the publisher, except in the case of brief quotations embodied in critical articles and reviews.

ACKNOWLEDGMENTS

Antiphon: We Illuminate a Night Scene in King Rene's Book of Love
Barrow Street: Self-Portrait as a Cup of Coffee
Blue Nib: Though I Avoided His Name, We Talked Our Truths into the Night
Crab Orchard Review: The Hinged Heart
Green Briar Review: Danger Keep off Submerged Objects; Give Me a Break When I See Myself as Her Again
Gris-Gris: Like Light in a Basin
Hamline Lit Link: The Unsolved Departure of the Common X
Journal of New Jersey Poets: The Chapter in Which the Moon Was Forgiven
Kelsey Review: Vultures
Ninth Letter: Doorknobs (as Fear Doorknobs)
Number One: How It Happens
Oddball: Something about Affection; Something Else about Affection
One: Binary
Open: Journal of Arts & Letters. Leaves Fall like Lapsarians
Postcard Poems and Prose: Spat
Redheaded Stepchild: Abduction of Sorts
River Heron Review: Several Months before You Were Born I Married a Man Who Wasn't Your Father
Shot Glass: The Cosmologist on His Divorce
Tar River Review: Vortex
Terrain: Once in Baltic, Ohio
Visions International: No Rock Bottom
West Trade Review: Credo
Zingara: It's Not Simple, the Heart—

Publisher: Leah Huete de Maines
Editor: Christen Kincaid
Cover Art: *Bluebird Argument* by Sheila Brown
Author Photo: Mark Hilringhouse
Cover Design: Elizabeth Maines McCleavy

Order online: www.finishinglinepress.com
also available on amazon.com

Author inquiries and mail orders:
Finishing Line Press
PO Box 1626
Georgetown, Kentucky 40324
USA

Table of Contents

Spat

Spat 1
Give Me a Break 2
That First Marriage 4
The Unsolved Departure of the Common X 5
The Cosmologist on His Divorce 6
Danger Keep Off Submerged Objects 7
Doorknobs 9
No Rock Bottom 10
Tornado Tongue 12
Spurned 13
Something about Marriage 14
Binary 15
Abduction of Sort 17
Though I Avoided His Name 18
Vortex 19

It's not simple, the heart—

It's not simple, the heart— 23
Once in Baltic Ohio 24
The Chapter in Which the Moon Was Forgiven 25
Several Months Before You Were Born, I Married
    a Man Who Wasn't Your Father 26
When I See Myself as Her Again 27
Self-Portrait as a Cup of Coffee 28
We Talked Our Truths into the Night 29
Something about Affection 30
Something Else about Affection 31
Like Light in a Basin 32
We Illuminate a Night Scene from King Rene's
    Book of Love 33
Vultures 34
Leaves Fall like Lapsarians 35
Credo 36

Spat

*for Lee
my one and only
spat-mate*

Spat

Afterwards . . . like post-party wine glasses,
collecting them, carrying them to the kitchen, washing
them up, and then the next morning finding one more
and then another on the book case, under the rocker,
and all the time thinking how Emily Dickinson
described her eyes, *like the Sherry in the Glass*
that the Guest leaves, and shouldn't she always treat him
as a guest, the guest of her heart? and yet another in the bedroom
on the night stand, his side of the bed, a guest, her guest,
her ever faithful guest, more or less, and why does she always ask,
couldn't you have carried it to the sink?

Give Me a Break

At first as dawn *slits*,
Later, as storm.

Lightning, those cadenzas
between the sheets.

I couldn't *shear off*
smoking.

Like a dolphin
splitting the water, desire.

My plain *broken*
by your complicated hills.

Fields, meadows,
nets.

Love, love
and then you *broke* my serve.

When I talked,
you *interrupted*.

Just once
to finish your sentence.

Oh, the sentence,
not unlike a posted ban.

You filched volume three
of the *Encyclopedia Britannica*.

You *broke* faith
like daily bread.

I *sliced* my shillings like pies,
broke you off pieces.

The branch from the wind-blown oak,
charred to warm your heart.

The femur *cracked*
running your way.

Our story *broke* in the evening news,
how I was found, tied and gagged.

Records, *shattered*.
CD, gummed.

Connection, gone.
What is there to fix?

That First Marriage

was the second and the third
and the present, my ex

somehow my ex again.
We managed

a serial nesting, monogamy
slipping from one state

to the next
like a line of dominoes

wending from Wyoming,
Michigan, Maine—

to that menagerie
in Nebraska,

a masquerade thrall
one more guise

to slip, one more snake
beginning.

I don't know how to define
our hide and tweak,

but now I find you
in the kitchen, making soup

without a recipe, skimming
the foam from the broth.

The Unsolved Departure of the Common X

It had been a long night on the beat
and a long walk back to the tall house
where the gumshoe took himself to sleep.

And when he stumbled in, he crawled
to bed without noticing the rope
with a name scrawled

in its loops. The practical joke
of her goodbye? The diary he copped?

She had been gone fourteen tears
and still had a secret life under wraps.
How else to explain her perfume floating

down the hemp. He sat down, caressed the loops,
and pulled out the sentence. "Dear Joe," it began.
"Dear Joe" as he began to smoke.

The Cosmologist on His Divorce

We drifted apart
like two galaxies.

Neither of us accelerated,
and yet we separated—

at first not understanding
the cosmos itself

was expanding
and there was no way

we could leap the light years
back.

Danger Keep Off Submerged Objects
Beach Sign, Sea Isle, NJ

Sign without punctuation:
without hesitant colon
comma coughing caveat
so
I ask the gulls how
the miller's daughter can spin
flaw into gold. Everything's hidden,
suggests the ring-billed beak
standing his house
on sand.

But there's a man
skimming the shore with a straw detector,
looking for danger.
Think the queer motions
of a faith healer
floating his hands over a body,
or a monarch curing scrofula,
the royal touch–
Doesn't seems to be
finding much–

We all hide something
but what did the king expect
when he took
the miller's chaff to bed.
Her face was her fortune
and that apparent.

Meanwhile the water shimmies
over itself,
sinking what
lies beneath,
the gold crucifix
some lost swimmer lost
with his faith.

Well, says my therapist friend,
the danger comes
when you start talking.

Repression keeps us going,
we stand on the rocks
we cannot bear.

The miller's daughter,
it is said,
did not mention Rumplestiltskin
after she said his name,
developed carpal tunnel syndrome
in his stead.

No more spinning for the queen.
Disease too
riddles our skins.
Tuberculosis.
That kind of danger deep beneath.

Doorknobs

Someday one will turn and slip—hot and heavy
        from your hand and you will hear
                its twin clunk on the other side of the bedroom

and there will be the door between the two of you,
        as it has been, apparently, before
            you noticed

and you will wish, since you are the wishing sort
        that you had the skill, mechanical or social,
            to slip knobs, grease locks.

You haven't been drinking, so it isn't the gin
        that keeps you from sliding the spindle back
            through the spindle hub.

It's ignorance—you don't even know
        the rod in your hand
            is called a spindle.

Stupid you, mistaking
        a cell phone
            for a doorknob.

You don't understand what you have done
        until the fireman bashes
            down the door

and then what to say?
        How could you have guessed
            your whole house was burning?

No Rock Bottom

You sink again
as the dying
sink into sheets,
as cowboys sink
into quick sand
which itself is
neither quick
nor dead,
merely inanimate,
particles
suspended
in sluice,
upward
flowing
waters
that only
beg your weight
to equal their own.
You remember
reading
you should swim
or is it float
on your back?
So lean back,
take deep breaths,
do nothing
fast,
but now you
are heavier
than usual,
what if this time
you can't
churn your way
up, out?

Others have panicked—
put rocks
in their pockets
before they started
for the river
where no man
steps
twice
yet you
seem to be
stepping
again,
the same river,
the same place
and
you suppose
eventually
you will
get up,
rise,
though this morning
even the sun
seems to be
sinking.

Tornado Tongue

But how could she stop the *rat a tat tattle*
in the brain, the hot-headed shatter of hard wood,
pileated spring drill, stiff skull and muscled neck,
splintered walnut, shattered eaves, dented cars
it's what language does with a long tongue,
batters the rail fence nail by nail, shatters the nests
of lesser birds, sprays debris, no way to keep out the rain—
who can forgive her? Who can not?

And so we divide ourselves into *pleases and don'ts*
while she considers us fodder for her tongue.

One day I saw a tiger cub paw a blackbird out of a bush,
strip its feathers with a lick, and there was the heart of the fledgling,
jammering like a jackhammer, trying to escape its chest.

I should have kissed her, wrote Hardy,
if the rain had lasted a minute more.

I should have kissed her.

Spurned

Plum days it's nothing more than a pit
in the corneal epithelium as din sways

the power lines—you were talking to me,
weren't you? Something about the baffle of cards

shushing fortune, think flick my dice,
think snake eyes, you always had two

and you were saying the sky is blue
though I knew it was air between us.

Now you've shunted me so far off,
you've become the spidery satellite slinking

towards the edge of the universe.
I no longer hear you breathing

though sometimes I imagine a dreamy star,
one with the five-clawed paw a child

could draw. No, I don't want you back,
I want to stop seeing your low lies

on the horizon. Back here,
the black is clearing.

Something about Marriage

It's not that one morning you decide
to walk out of your little house—

the cabin at the edge of the Minnesota woods
or the semi-detached in rural New Jersey—

and go into the cold in your thin cotton gown
and calloused feet,

it's the chill that slides into your kitchen
and stands behind you

as you measure out the coffee,
the nip that slips into the bedroom as you bend to smooth the sheets,

like one of those ghosts you've dreamed
wafting down the corridor

at the mental hospital, the sudden rush
of cold that makes you know

how solitary you are. And you are not sure
if the icy wraith is telling you something you already guessed

or if this is a revelation:
the fire in the hearth

which you have imagined flickering all these years
is gone.

Of course, sometimes like frost
the chill is brief.

Binary

In those days there were two of us,
sometimes you were the one

sometimes me, though I often felt nothing,
you always on and I off or a little off,

a little young, a bit unready,
but we worked together, discovered,

how much we could generate,
and so it didn't seem complicated

to be separate, single, particulate,
lone star, odd star, one and only star,

in an empty universe.
Then we grew pods with little peas,

each a perfect zero, off and ought, on or naught.
The power of nothing did its simple addition

under the trees, the grass nixed the morning sun,
it was just one great zippo everyday

while our children, our two and only,
played baseball from dawn to nil,

Zip the bat, Zilch the ball
from early moon until zero,

we switched them now and then
like bubbles, watched them pop

in and out of existence though our best psychologists
said this was more about sex than numbers.

At night they conspired to seethe
like two steam engines,

puffing their little ciphers
up and down the track.

Abduction of Sorts

It doesn't happen
as the tabloids urge,
the brittle hair
slicing the kid's forehead,
the knife, the knee.
No chokeholds
or throwdowns
in the forest of solitary trees,
no lunchbox found still smelling
of peanut butter and jelly.
No roller skates
rumbling the uneven sidewalk,
and then the uneven screech of brakes.
No bicycle repainted red.
No. Children,
most of them,
do not leave suddenly—
they laze out the open door
and turn around
with smiles as idle
as red balloons,
but when they return
in a year or two
they are not
what they used to be,
now strange,
perhaps deflated,
vulnerable
and we wonder
what happened
on that amble
past the parking lot
we thought was empty
except for them.

Though I Avoided His Name

Night drove out from under
his soiled baseball cap

into the limestone west,
into the saffron and ochre sunstone

towards Black Rock, Arizona,
passing through the Pleasantvilles

one by one: New Jersey,
New York, Pennsylvania,

Ohio, Indiana, Iowa,
Texas, Wisconsin.

And I was sitting beside him
once again . . .

tossing my clothes
out the window.

Vortex

Nothing stays
where you put it.
True, no one stole
the mole you left
spinning on your shoulder
while you spent
that sunny year in Tuscany.
But, right, it wasn't a mole,
it was a Nissan,
the cheap one
with plastic skin
and a rubbery
manual shifter.
And it wasn't Tuscany,
it was that cheap package deal—
five days in family-
friendly Cancun.
Yet, you went
and returned,
and the car
was still here.
Next time—
if there is
a next time—
the car may flotsam its way
to that plastic dump
in the middle
of the Pacific,
half the size
of Mexico.

It's not simple, the heart—

It's not simple, the heart—

artery-fisted, three-pronged aorta
with its middle finger twisted up

yours and better be. *Brachiocephaliac*
to the right, left *common carotid* in the middle,

and left, the *left subclavian*: the blood-draggled glove
of a penniless troll, the knot

of a neglected vegetable, fennel, celeriac,
but the heart always left, left behind,

left below, and common, that too,
the neck, the head, and left again,

and yet it keeps on beating, who could guess?
Drum and drum skin, thick stick, complicit.

The complicated heart because complexity's simpler
than simplicity? Think Bach:

his great heart with *mitral* and *aortic* valves all throbbing,
oh who loves him more than I, this year

when no one is performing Brandenburgs in public,
nothing now but the sound of the recorded heart,

played to calm an infant, sound's knotted beauty,
septum, septum, do you not love the *septum,*

the separation, the beat between the beats,
dirt clot and fairy tubules, clenched face of an infant

dismissing what fed him, the ventricles, the valves—
the Greeks thought we think with the heart.

The heart's a hollow muscle.
Some days I want to think with mine too.

Once in Baltic, Ohio

I was a shallow girl in the flooding dusk
unaware of the depth of things,

my grandmother floating beside me on the high porch,
the swing chains shiny and creaking

and I heard
the mockingbird's gutturals in the husky pear

without understanding how a bird
might claim his own solitude

in the vowels of another, and then it happened:
night with all its pins began

pricking the dusk as my grandmother had pricked my belly
as she adjusted the waist of the new dress she was making for me,

every star needled its individual jeer
and the moon poked its curved thorn

until the little pond below became so still
I knew I could climb onto the porch railing

and spiral down into its darkness, its body becoming my body,
and never touch bottom.

The Chapter in Which the Moon Was Forgiven

My mother preferred periods to semicolons.
You can't stop smoking halfway, she said.
It's cease or ampersand. When she found
my *buts* and *run-ons* in the attic, she burned them
sentence by sentence in the big oil drum. Lascivious,
she would have said, had she tried such tokes.
Ignited my father's love letters too, logs
punctuated long before she smoldered along,
seems there was a red-haired nurse
who wouldn't follow him to Pittsburgh.
How much does a preacher make? Not enough,
he sighed. My mother found those epistles
in the back of his drawer, read them pilcrow by pilcrow,
and then they disappeared. You just keep
those periods coming, she told me, dousing my pants.

Several Months Before You Were Born, I Married a Man Who Wasn't Your Father
title of sculpture by Lynden Cline

So listen: *your* father was sweeter than Jesus
but he fluxed the Ford, trying to grab the rattles
gloating in the frame. If he had been meaner

he would have shaken the throats
of those kids chattering in the balcony
while he was preaching to the scold-maids.

Off course, they squirmed away too,
every one of them with his loaves and his fishes,
and he couldn't marry me, no, not ever.

You've had five husbands, he said,
like that Samaritan woman,
and the man you're living with now

isn't. Didn't turn out well either for that Magdalene
kneeling beside me those stark Sunday mornings,
something about the windows, stained.

What else could I do but find someone
who could fix transmissions?
As for that half-yours sister Mary

I paid her off with starlight mints
to keep her singing Galilee.
So come back here and pick up the chair.

I named you Forgiveness
but your nickname is Angie,
short for Anger.

When I See Myself as Her Again

She is wearing a white dress
with puffy blue rainclouds
and sequined raindrops.
She has her hair cut pixie
and her legs have lengthened
though her hands hang at her sides,
wishing, I think, to tug
at her Peter Pan collar.
I think of my mother,
the way her hands hung
when she was forced to pose.
So it's Sunday again,
the day I am supposed
to feel Jesus the way
my sister does, her face my face
singing *Such as I Am*
beside me, the white blouse
with its Peter Pan collar,
the blue plaid skirt
with its fluffy pleats,
the wide black cinch belt.
I remember her face again
in Rome when I stand
before St. Theresa in Ecstasy,
and wonder why another's self feels
things my self can't.

Later she appears
in a hot pink halter dress,
her signature smile
paired with her sky-high
Jimmy Choo peep-toes.
I didn't know you at first,
I say as if I catch herself
in my mirror.

Self-Portrait as a Cup of Coffee

A bit like the one I made this morning, not bad, but not good.

Not good as a child is good by everyone's standards but my mother's. She dressed me up for Halloween in a nursery frock of her contrivance, red and white cotton, laced and ribboned.

I was fat then and I was good, but chubby, and that was good then. I ate my broccoli, which was not very good. I hated it.

My mother made that curl—you know the rhyme—right in the middle of my forehead.

Until then I didn't know she thought me horrid, a bitter lesson, bitter as coffee before I knew coffee was good.

My mother thought me horrid—like David Trimble who sat across from me in third grade kicking until my shins were bruised.

He was horrid.

Mrs. Cohen sat him there because she knew I was good, too shy to complain.

It was horrid—being that sort of child, that sort of coffee, bitter, good, but not really.

We talked our truths into the night
Coleen Marks

Into darkness. The way truth with its spotty light
bounces off the river birch at the edge of the lot,

river birch bifurcating, one truth becomes two,
spur-like, two-leaved, the beginning of a book,

such an easy lateral branching, and then pages
and pages drift back and forth in the night air.

I tell you my disappointments, those black lenticels
begun long ago, things I tried to scratch out,

into another heart, into heartwood. How long it has been
since we heard from the children, the boy, the girls,

sitting perhaps somewhere like us talking their own scars
into the dusk? Into the gloom?

Some say it is easier to speak
when we cannot see the other's mouth.

I say some nights I cannot stop speaking
volumes into the sunfall, the dark stars.

Something about Affection

We are walking
in the meadow

when a rabbit leaps
between your legs,

and you feel his fur
brush your calves

and I imagine
I feel it too.

Something Else about Affection

You have a right hand
and a wrong
like a man playing hearts.

The Queen of Spades
wants everything
as queens often do.

You don't like games
though you came from
a family of card sharks.

Rook was your poker,
no money, just nasty bickering
about bad plays.

It's a how you learn
another's moves—
how you learn to lose.

Like Light in a Basin
Appalachian Trail, 2009

All that night we seemed to be slouching
toward something mirrored in the scatter of water,
a moon, perhaps, wrapped in a papery mist
though the moon itself seemed to follow us

as if it were the bony dog we left behind.
When at last we cramped down in the leaves
it was raining, soft and amber, and we began
to dream as if we had left nothing,

not even certainty, behind in the sweat.
I suppose it was then that the stars began
to float on the brow of the pools,

then that you rose and left me there
to dream a little longer. When I woke
there was nothing to eat, nothing to wear.

We Illuminate a Night Scene from King René's *Book of Love*

You are standing in the stern of a painted boat where no one sits—
this is the way with knights, their armor does not gleam
and your leg, if it still exists, cramps at the shin.

Ahead the darkness grinds, the jagged water, the jagged isle,
and you are sick of the sea and sick of your page Desire
with his mute tunic and his sky full of metal stars.

You see the woman who has hung her candle in the canvas tent,
I am the woman at the edge of her wick, the one angling a silver nail—
she lifts the fish out of the water and turns towards your lips.

You come ashore without knowing how I came there,
for this is the dark page in Love's domain,
and instead of bright bread she gives you a biscuit.

It tastes of the roasted fish called Farewell
and her salad she calls Sweet Reply, it is all you can eat today,
Friday, and a fast day in *The Book of Love*.

Vultures

They disappear for days,
the blue-enamel heaven
empty as a pot,
no ripe meat
rising in the kettle,
no random reek.
The canal where we walk
scrubbed of duckweed,
vegetable protein rot.

Then they return
wheeling the steeple,
cadaverine
putrescine
rising on the wind,
great trundles reminding
some somewhere
something is dying,
dead, climatic shift,
black plague.
We sniff our breath,
our armpits,
whiff nothing yet.

Leaves Fall like Lapsarians

During July, August, too early for grace
the willful ones, wily goats, the desperate
refuse to live. You see them, a leaf,
a lamina, disobedient maple, wild cherry

crimson before its time, you can't blame
it on sex, you can't blame it on women,
the early falls for which there is no explanation—
the child who tumbles off his tricycle

and inexplicably dies, you understand
a lightning bolt, the slow rust in Eden, but this?
Nearby the yellow pines with their fidgety needles
sew aprons, something to breech

the tumble to dust. The heat increases.
The cicadas begin their noisome hum.
It's in the air. The end, but not the end of time.
Not yet. Keep me as the apple of your eye.

Credo

I believe in space
the way lovers loosen
time.

Let their arms stretch,
let the legs begin
their leave,

for what are we
if we cannot return
to where we were.

Not that we will see
the same red giants
and white dwarfs.

Even as we seem
to join
we separate.

If continuum,
the meteor—
if nostalgia, star-stuff.

No more touching
should we forget
which planets spin

and which wrinkle.
There's Mercury
above our bed

still shrinking
with the semblance
of who we were.

www.ingramcontent.com/pod-product-compliance
Lightning Source LLC
LaVergne TN
LVHW041557070426
835507LV00011B/1143